PEOPLE IN THE PAST

Ancient Greek War and Weapons

Haydn Middleton

Heinemann Library
Chicago, Illinois

Text and cover designed by Tinstar
Originated by Ambassador Litho
Printed in China by WKT

07 06 05 04
10 9 8 7 6 5 4 3 2

Library of Congress Cataloging-in-Publication Data

Middleton, Haydn.
 Ancient Greek War and Weapons / Haydn Middleton.
    p. cm. -- (People in the past)
Includes bibliographical references and index.
Summary: Presents an overview of war in ancient Greece, including
noteworthy wars, weaponry, types of fighting, and the importance of
warfare in ancient Greek society.
 ISBN 1-58810-635-7
 1. Military art and science--Greece--History--Juvenile literature. 2.
Naval art and science--Mediterranean Region--Juvenile literature. 3.
Military history, Ancient--Juvenile literature. 4. Naval history,
Ancient--Juvenile literature. [1. Military art and
science--Greece--History. 2. Naval art and science--Greece--History. 3.
Weapons, Ancient--Greece. 4. Greece--History--To 146 B.C.] I. Title.
II. Series.
 U33 .M54 2002
 355'.00938--dc21

                                        2001005134

Acknowledgments
The Publishers would like to thank the following for permission to reproduce photographs: AKG
London/Erich Lessing pp. 6, 18, 23, 38; Acropolis Museum, p. 7; Ancient Art & Architecture
Collection, pp. 8, 12, 20, 22, 24, 26, 30, 32, 34, 36, 41; C. M. Dixon, pp. 10, 16, 21, 30, 40; AKG
London/British Museum, p. 14; Ashmolean Museum, p. 24; Werner Forman Archive, p. 37; Werner
Forman Archive/N. J. Saunders, p. 42.
Cover photograph reproduced with permission of Photo Archive.

Every effort has been made to contact copyright holders of any material reproduced in this book.
Any omissions will be rectified in subsequent printings if notice is given to the publisher.

Some words are shown in bold, **like this.** You can find out what they mean by looking
in the glossary.

Contents

The World of the Ancient Greeks

▶ ◀▶ ◀▶ ◀▶ ◀▶ ◀▶ ◀▶ ◀▶ ◀▶ ◀▶ ◀▶ ◀▶ ◀▶ ◀▶ ◀▶ ◀▶ ◀▶ ◀

When people talk about ancient Greece, they do not just mean the modern-day country of Greece as it used to be. The ancient Greek world was made up of the hot, rocky mainland of Greece and hundreds of islands in the Aegean, Ionian, and Adriatic Seas, as well as further settlements overseas, in places ranging from northern Africa to what we now call Turkey and Italy. The earliest Greek speakers did not think that they all belonged to a single country. For a long time, they did not even think that they all belonged to the same **civilization.**

The ancient Greeks built one of the most creative civilizations ever seen. It was also one of the most warlike. Power was held by a number of city-states. The Greek word for a city-state is *polis.* Each *polis* controlled the villages and farmland around it. These fiercely independent city-states, or *poleis,* had their own laws and customs, yet were seldom able to live in peace together. In the words of modern historian Oliver Taplin, "the history of Greece is largely a history of war," even though some of these wars did not last for very long.

The Greeks did not just fight among themselves. They invaded lands in Europe, Asia, and Africa, in their quest for trade, precious metals, and slaves. Sometimes they even managed to fight on the same side, to defend their common Greek homeland against foreign invaders such as the **Persians.** From this experience, they formed a low opinion of the military skills of foreigners, all of whom they called **barbarians.** The Greeks believed that only Greek men knew how to fight with true courage and discipline.

From Minoans to Macedonians

For centuries, the mightiest people in the Greek world were the Minoans, based on the island of Crete. Power then passed to the warlike Mycenaeans, based on the mainland, in the region known as the **Peloponnese.** This was followed, around 1100 B.C.E., by centuries of confusion and upheaval, but since the art of writing was also lost, we know very little about it. Later, in the Classical Age, from about

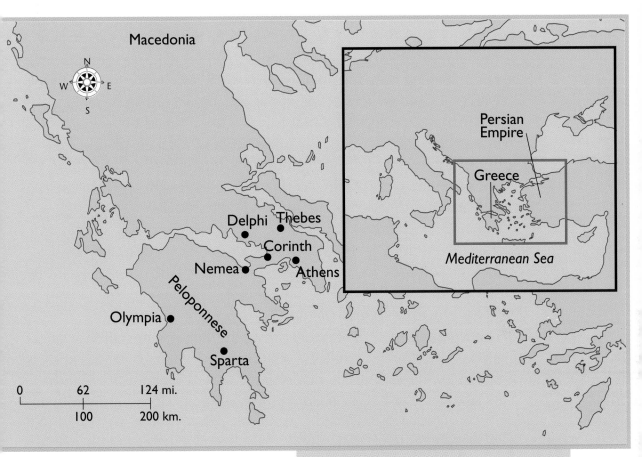

500 B.C.E. until about 300 B.C.E., prosperity was restored by the rise of many city-states, including Athens, Sparta, and Thebes. Most of the information in this book is about life in such city-states during this period of Greek history.

Ancient Greece was not a single, unified country but was instead a collection of many separate states that often waged war on one another. The ancient Greeks used the word *Hellas* to mean all the places where there was a Greek way of life.

The city-states all had their own ways of life and sometimes had their own ways of fighting, too. They were, however, united by the Greek language and their belief that their ways were superior to those of any foreign barbarians. Whether or not that was true, ancient Greek words, ideas, art forms, and attitudes still have a deep effect on us all today.

War in the Greek World

Each Greek city-state wanted to be powerful. It aimed to be seen as the leading state in its region—on land or sea—or even in the whole of Greece. This often meant waging wars. The Athenian historian Thucydides said that his own people had three main reasons for fighting: First, to win honor and respect; second, to enrich themselves by seizing **loot** from their enemies; and third, because they were afraid. All the city-states fought partly because of fear. They dreaded being invaded by **barbarian** foreign armies or being conquered by a neighboring Greek city-state. So they stayed constantly ready to defend themselves, and sometimes, if they sensed they were in danger, they struck first.

"The glorious deeds of men"

Thucydides wrote eight books about the **Peloponnesian** War of 431–404 B.C.E. This struggle for supremacy between Athens and Sparta ended in Sparta's victory, with Athens losing more than half its **citizens.** Just before this time, the historian Herodotus wrote an

Warfare in ancient times was bloody and brutal. Once battle began, large numbers of lives could be lost as the army of one state aimed to prove its superiority over the other.

Athena, the Greek goddess of war, mourns soldiers lost in battle.

account of the earlier wars between the Greeks and **Persians.** He was the first man to call his work history. The Greek word *historia* means questions, and Herodotus was interested in recording answers to people's questions about how the wars were won. Thucydides was interested in more than telling people about war victories. He looked deeper and found problems. He showed how, under the stress of conflict, people behaved in different and often unacceptable ways. "Even the meanings of words," he wrote, "are changed. Reckless daring is believed to be loyal courage.... The lover of violence is always trusted and his opponent suspected."

"Kudos" and loss

Between 500 and 300 B.C.E., Athens was at war for two of every three years. Many Greek vases show a soldier preparing to go to war. Warfare was seen as a noble, manly pursuit. The fame and glory that were won in wartime were called kudos. We still use the word today, to mean the credit that you earn for doing something good. Warfare was also tragic in ancient times. When many young warriors died in Samos, the Athenian statesman Pericles declared, "It was as if the spring had been taken from the year." He meant that the warriors had been young men, and that the city would be weakened by losing men who could have become great artists, athletes, politicians, or **philosophers.**

The Greatest War of All

In ancient times, the city of Troy stood on the west coast of what is now Turkey. About a century ago, its ruins were discovered and **excavated** by archaeologists. Some historians believe that the city was destroyed by a Greek fleet and army in about 1210 B.C.E. The ancient Greeks had many legends about a war against Troy. Around 800 to 700 B.C.E., the poet Homer recorded some of these legends in his long poem, the *Iliad*. We know very little about Homer. He may not even have written the poem himself, but instead may have passed it on **orally** to others.

This painting shows the legendary Greek hero Achilles in one of his battle frenzies. In the *Iliad*, Homer described how Achilles "stormed all over the field like some inhuman being, drawing men on and killing them. And the black earth ran with blood."

A source and an influence

The *Iliad* describes the fighting at Troy. For nine years, according to legend, the Greeks **besieged** the city without success. Then, in the tenth year, it fell because of a trick. The Greeks pretended to give up and left behind a huge wooden horse. Thinking it was a religious offering, the Trojans dragged it inside their walls. Greek warriors were hidden in the horse, and they sprang out and ransacked the city. This event may never have actually happened. Throughout Homer's poem, however, there are many details about ancient Greek weapons and armor that are useful to historians.

The *Iliad* had a huge effect on later writers and artists. According to the *Aeneid,* by the Roman poet Virgil, a survivor of the Trojan War rebuilt Troy at Rome. Ancient Greek soldiers were heavily influenced by the Trojan war legends, which they knew as well as we know stories about World War I and World War II. Their own dreams were the same as those of the warriors at Troy—to win eternal fame for great military deeds.

Alexander and Achilles

Among the many ancient people influenced by the legendary Trojan War was Alexander the Great. He conquered a vast empire that stretched deep into Asia from his native Greek-speaking kingdom of Macedonia. His own hero was the mighty warrior Achilles, the most effective fighter in Homer's poem. In 334 B.C.E., Alexander paid homage at a tomb that was supposed to mark the Greek warrior's resting place. He is also said to have carried a copy of the *Iliad* with him as he fought his way as far east as the Indus River in modern Pakistan. Alexander was a great warrior, as Achilles was, but he also died young.

Who Were the Greek Warriors?

The Greeks loved to tell war stories featuring **aristocrats**—kings and princes. Often these heroes were pitted against each other in single combat, and sometimes these contests could turn the tide of a whole battle.

Real-life warfare in ancient Greece was a different matter. Many Greek soldiers were just citizens who took up arms when war broke out. You will find out a lot about them on the following pages. They fought not as individuals but instead fought shoulder to shoulder, as fellow **citizens,** showing great bravery and discipline in defense of their communities.

War-torn Greece

Herodotus, who is sometimes called the first historian ever, recorded a sad proverb: "In peace, sons bury their fathers; in war, fathers bury their sons." War, in other words, can change the normal way of things. The Greeks liked to think of peacetime as more normal than wartime, but they still spent a lot of time fighting. Reminders of war were

Dating from about 490 B.C.E., this vase, from Athens, is one of many from ancient Greece that show preparations for battle. The central soldier is arming himself.

everywhere, too—in theater performances, the tombs of the dead, victory monuments, and the sculptures that stood in temples. In some private houses, arms and armor were hung on the walls, and bowls and cups were decorated with scenes of battles.

Why did the Greeks fight so much? According to Thucydides, the Athenian historian, "We believe that it is divine, and know for certain that it is universally human … to rule whatever one can." The city-states fought against invading **barbarians** for the right to rule over themselves, and fought among one another for leadership over all or part of Greece. This gave Greek warriors many chances to win glory on the battlefield. Some of them became very famous. After a great victory over the **Persians** in 490 B.C.E., the men who fought at Marathon were remembered as an inspiration by generations of Athenians. At the battle of Thermopylae, in 480 B.C.E., one thousand Spartans won lasting fame for defending a mountain pass in central Greece against a far larger Persian force.

A soldier's life

Greek writings from ancient times tell us how people felt about fighting. Part-time soldiers fought bravely for their city-states but had families back at home to worry about. These families expected them to return in glory. Less heroic warriors, accepting that a battle was lost, sometimes threw down their shields and ran. The poet Archilochus did not regret the loss of a perfect shield that he left behind on the battlefield: "Some enemy now has the use of it, but I have saved my life. What care I for that shield? One day I'll buy another, just as good."

The Persian Wars

Under Cyrus the Great, who lived from about 585 to about 529 B.C.E., the **Persian** Empire grew and absorbed the eastern half of the Greek world. Darius I conquered the Greek states of Thrace, Scythia, and Macedonia, and was determined to conquer the southern regions of Greece too. Then, the Greeks of Ionia rose in revolt against him. In 498 B.C.E., the Athenians sent some warships to assist them. They could not help the Ionians to secure their freedom. The Greeks managed to burn Sardis, the Persian capital city. Darius vowed to take revenge. He ordered his **majordomo** to tell him three times a day to "remember the Athenians." That is why Herodotus later wrote that the Athenian ships of 498 B.C.E. "were the beginning of evils for both Greeks and **barbarians**."

The Greeks pool their resources

In 490 B.C.E., Darius sent a huge army, said to have been 100,000 strong, to attack the Greek coast. The Athenians opposed them on the plain of Marathon with a tenth as many men, yet somehow they managed to overcome them. **Casualty** figures in ancient times were often exaggerated by historians on the side of the victors, but 6,400 Persians were said to have been killed, with only 192 Greeks said to have lost their lives.

This wine vase from the 4th century B.C.E. shows Greek and Persian soldiers engaged in single combat. Greek artists often showed noble Greek warriors fighting naked, while their barbarian enemies were shown clothed and wearing protective armor.

Darius died before he could attack Greece again. His son Xerxes took up the cause and invaded in 480 B.C.E. with an army that, according to one Greek writer, was made up of five million men. By contrast, only about 250,000 people lived in the whole densely populated region of Attica, where Athens is located. A number of city-states joined forces to oppose them, but they were powerless to prevent a Persian victory at Thermopylae. The Persians then burned Athens to the ground, but they were defeated at sea in the battle of Salamis and, finally, in 479 B.C.E., on land in the battle of Plataea.

By pulling together, the Greeks had fended off the Persian threat. They felt that they were helped by their superior political system. For they were free men, unlike the Persians, who had to obey an **autocratic** ruler. As an exiled Spartan told Xerxes, the Greeks obeyed only their own laws, not any human master.

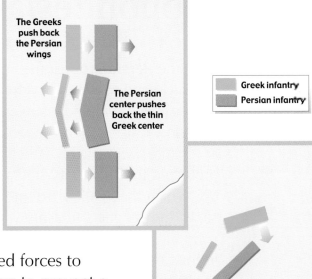

The Greeks push back the Persian wings

The Persian center pushes back the thin Greek center

Greek infantry
Persian infantry

The Greek wings attack the center

At the battle of Marathon, in 490 B.C.E., the heavily outnumbered Greeks won by attacking the wings (the side sections, as shown by arrows) and trapping many Persians who had broken through at the center.

Hubris

Many Greeks believed in the idea of *hubris.* This meant that rich rulers would always strive to become greater, but then the gods would become envious and inevitably strike them down. Herodotus wrote that at the battle of Salamis "it was the Athenians who, *after the god*, repulsed the Persian king." By this, he meant that the Greek soldiers succeeded only because the gods had already decided that the mighty Persians should not have victory. "Do you see," asked Herodotus, "how it is always the greatest houses and the tallest trees that the god hurls his thunderbolts at?"

The Peloponnesian War

After the **Persian** invasions, more than 200 Greek city-states and islands joined together in a new anti-Persian alliance, to raid the **barbarians'** own lands. Since its headquarters were on the island of Delos, it was called the Delian League. Gradually it turned into an empire, with mighty Athens at its head. The Athenians protected the other city-states and in return made them pay a tax, which they called "tribute," to finance this protection. In 454 B.C.E., the League's treasury was moved from Delos to Athens.

In the absence of a serious threat of attack from abroad, some of the city-states began to resent the power that Athens had over them. Sparta, in the southern region known as the **Peloponnese,** was particularly opposed. Finally, Sparta joined with other like-minded city-states to put an end to the wealth and power of Athens. After forming the Peloponnesian League, they declared war on Athens in 431 B.C.E.

This bust shows the Athenian statesman Pericles, wearing his general's helmet. In the Golden Age of Athens, under his direction, some of the city's greatest buildings were constructed.

The twenty-seven-year nightmare

At first there was a **stalemate** in the war. Athens could not be defeated at sea, while Sparta could not be defeated on land. The Athenians seemed safe behind their great defenses, but an outbreak of plague in 430–429 B.C.E. struck down many of their leading men, including Pericles. Under his successor, Cleon, there were terrible brutalities. When Melos revolted against Athens, the Athenians responded by killing the men of the Melos and enslaving the women and children and Melos. When the Spartans captured Plataea, they too carried out mass slaughter.

Finally, in 415 B.C.E. and 405 B.C.E., the Athenians suffered two disastrous naval defeats. Helped by Persian money, in 404 B.C.E. the Spartans captured Athens and then took over their empire. Maybe they suffered from **hubris** too. In 371 B.C.E. and 362 B.C.E. the Spartans in turn were overcome by the armies of Thebes. The balance of power was constantly shifting in the Greece of the quarrelsome city-states.

Powerful Pericles

From 463 B.C.E. to 429 B.C.E., the most important man in Athens was Pericles. He came to power after the defeat of the Persians and played a major part in the development of Athenian **democracy.** He was a great **orator,** but many comic plays of the time made fun of him. He died in the plague that hit Athens soon after the Peloponnesian War broke out. "He was able to control the multitude in a free spirit," wrote Thucydides. "He led them rather than was led by them." His war strategy for Athens was to avoid land battles and to make seaborne attacks on the Peloponnese, so that the strength of the Spartans would gradually be reduced.

Magnificent Macedonians

While the city-states were at war with each other, a new mighty power, known as Macedonia, arose on the wild northern borders of Greece. Its people did not all speak Greek, and they were ruled over by kings. From 359 B.C.E., their monarch was Philip II, who proved to be one of history's great generals. He trained a large full-time army to fight for him with utter devotion. His **infantry** were armed with a thrusting **pike,** or *sarissa,* that could be more than 16 1/2 feet (5 meters) long. They formed "Macedonian **phalanxes,**" which were densely packed squares of warriors carrying shields for protection and bristling with spears. These were linked up with fast-moving, highly-disciplined **cavalry.**

Philip's first goal was to unite all the Greek city-states under Macedonian rule. He succeeded, finally crushing a city-state alliance at Chaeronea in 338 B.C.E. His next aim was to invade Persia. This was in revenge, he claimed, for the **Persian** invasion of Greece 150 years before. In 336 B.C.E., however, he was stabbed to death by a young bodyguard named Pausanias. "Nothing has changed," said the son who succeeded him, "except the name of the king." The new king's name was Alexander, and in his reign of just less than thirteen years, he would achieve more than even Philip could have dreamed of achieving.

Made some time between 359 and 336 B.C.E., this Greek coin features Philip II racing a chariot. It celebrates the king's great success in the Olympic Games of 356 B.C.E. As a military and sports hero, he was a great inspiration to his people.

An empire in three continents

The map below shows Alexander the Great's triumphant trail of conquest. Setting out with an army of 30,000 infantry and 5,000 cavalry, not only did he defeat the Persians in 334 B.C.E. at the Granicus River but he then marched onward to overcome Tyre, Egypt, and the eastern part of the Persian Empire. Marching still farther onward, into India, he seized the Kingdom of Poros in 326 B.C.E. Even his loyal troops were too weary to expand his empire any farther after that. Soldiers were paid from the **loot** that was seized as they went. All along his route, Alexander founded cities where **Hellenistic,** or Greek-style, civilization then took root. Already a legend, he died in Babylon in 323 B.C.E. at the age of 32 years.

Godlike conqueror

Alexander was a brilliant general. He led his armies over vast distances at great speed, but always kept up their **morale.** Alexander was a master at devising the right tactics for each battle that they fought. He saw himself as almost mythical and encouraged the people of his enormous empire to worship and adore him like a god. The earliest surviving accounts of his life date from Roman times, several centuries after he died, so we cannot be sure how Alexander intended to run his empire. We do know that he was not narrow-minded: he gave jobs to Persians as well as Greeks and adopted some Persian customs.

This map shows the enormous empire conquered by Alexander the Great.

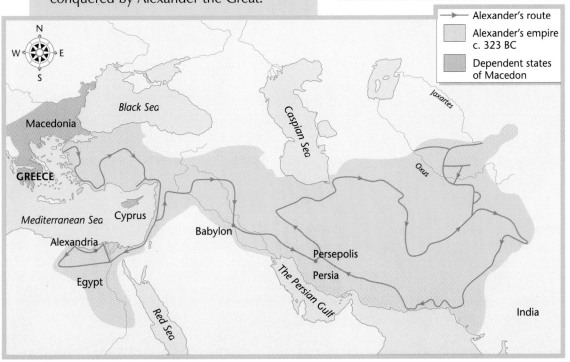

Alexander's route

Alexander's empire c. 323 BC

Dependent states of Macedon

17

The Citizen-Soldier

In ancient Greece, wars were not large in scale, but they could still be brutal. As the 5th century B.C.E. began, the armies of the city-states were quite small. Battles were dominated by foot soldiers called hoplites. These were fully armored spear carriers, whose main defense was a round wooden shield that was strengthened with bronze. In fact, they took their name from the Greek word for shield. The masters of hoplite warfare were the Spartans. Partly this was because of the strict way that future Spartan soldiers were brought up and trained. Elsewhere in Greece, hoplites were very much part-time, unprofessional soldiers.

These young hoplites are preparing themselves for battle. The warrior in the foreground is putting on one of his greaves, or shin guards. Some hoplites also wore padding beneath their greaves.

Who could be a hoplite?

Not every able-bodied man in a city-state fought as a hoplite. That honor was reserved for **citizens** from the upper and middle classes. Sometimes these men were called "those who provide their own shields"—in other words, they had to be weathy enough that they could supply their own weapons and armor.

As the Spartan poet Tyrtaeus put it, everyone admired "the young man who remains steadfast unceasingly in the front ranks." So there was little difficulty in enforcing the law that all adult male citizens had to serve as hoplites in times of war. In 5th-century-B.C.E. Athens, this was about one-third of the population. Except in Sparta, it was usually left up to the individual how much he trained. Some elite units, such the 300-strong Theban Sacred Band, did train together. In Athens, *ephebes,* who were from eighteen to twenty years of age, gained military experience by patrolling the countryside, and by the 330s B.C.E., they were trained in hoplite fighting for a full year, too.

Soldier behind a shield

The hoplite shield was round, 3 feet (about 1 meter) wide and weighed about 15 1/2 pounds (about 7 kilograms). The carrier wore it on his left, passing his arm through a ring to a grip held in the left hand. It covered most of the carrier's body and kept his right arm free to wield a thrusting spear that was 7 or 8 feet (2 or 2.5 meters) long. This spear was his main weapon, even though he carried a short sword too. On his head he wore a metal helmet, with body-armor called a **corselet** around his torso and shin guards called **greaves** on his legs. Although there were no modern-style "uniforms" in the early 5th century B.C.E., hoplites in the same army might carry a common "field sign." For instance, a helmet or shield painted in some distinguishing color. In the heat of battle, this would show them who was on their side.

Fighting in Formation

To stand any chance of success in battle, hoplites had to be brave and skilful. They also needed to be extremely well disciplined. Although their individual skills were vital, they were also part of a much larger team. The team that the hoplites fought in was called a **phalanx.**

All for one and one for all

Phalanxes were densely packed squares of warriors that advanced against each other at a running pace. For hoplites, their own shield would cover the left side, while their neighbor's shield gave some protection on the right side. Each phalanx was like a porcupine, bristling with spears. These were thrust forward in an orderly, overhand fashion. The moment of impact must have been awesome, as spear clashed with spear and as shield clashed with shield.

According to the historian Thucydides, every hoplite "brings his unprotected side as near as possible to the shield of the man drawn up on his right and believes that density of formation is the best protection." Once the formation broke, it was every man for himself.

If the hoplites in the first line fell, then those in the lines behind kept on coming forward to take over, trampling the dead and the wounded underfoot. Finally, when one phalanx broke and the surviving men inside it fled, the battle was over.

The Macedonian monarchs Philip II and Alexander the Great used their **infantry** in a different way. The soldiers in a Macedonian phalanx had longer spears and smaller shields than the Greek hoplites did. With regular training, the Macedonian infantry learned to be flexible in battle, although their main duty was to defend, not to attack. Sometimes their job was to pin down part of an enemy line, while the cavalry launched an attack on the flank or the rear. Just as in the city-states' armies, discipline was very important.

This is a lightly armed *peltast*—named after his oddly curved shield or *pelte*. *Peltasts* specialized in hit-and-run attacks on more heavily armed soldiers.

Monsters to the hoplites

In the mountainous northwestern part of Greece, the Thracians developed their own form of warfare. Sometimes city-states' armies had specialist warriors, called *peltasts*, play a supporting role in battles. Hoplites feared these lightly armed soldiers "as little children fear monsters," according to Xenophon, an ex-soldier who wrote history books. Equipped with a long javelin and a short sword, the *peltast* was protected only by a light shield of wicker or hide. This meant that they could run forward, throw their javelins, and then quickly dart back again. Sometimes the more heavily armed hoplites might try to chase them—and would fall out of formation and be picked off in hit-and-run attacks by other *peltasts*.

Spartan Soldiers

In the 5th century B.C.E., the warriors of one city-state had a reputation that was second to none. This was Sparta, where life was very different from elsewhere in ancient Greece. There, children became the state's property as soon as they were born. At seven years of age, boys were sent to a **barracks**-like boarding school, in which they not only were educated but also were trained for the hardships of war. They were allowed only one cloak a year, it was said, and they slept on rushes gathered from the river.

All male **citizens** became soldiers on leaving school, and they then had to devote all their time to the service of the city-state. If they married, they were not even allowed to live with their wives until they were 30 years old. Meanwhile, the Spartans' farming was done for them by **Helots,** previously conquered people who far outnumbered the Spartans themselves.

This statue now stands at Thermopylae as a memorial to the 1,000 Spartans and their king, Leonidas, who died here in a battle against the **Persians** in 480 B.C.E.

Human or beast?

In the words of historian Oliver Taplin, the Spartan warrior's purpose in life was "to be 1 of 10,000 identical component parts in a war machine." Many scholars and artists in other parts of ancient Greece disapproved of this single-mindedness. "It is the standards of civilized men not of beasts that must be kept in mind," wrote the **philosopher** and scientist Aristotle, "for it is good men not beasts who are capable of real courage. Those like the Spartans who concentrate on the one and ignore the other in their education turn men into machines." However, Sparta's own poet Tyrtaios expressed the Spartan ideal in this verse, when he encouraged all soldiers to be prepared to die gladly:

"Be brave, fear not the number of the enemy
Stand straight in the front of the
rank with your shield before you
and see your life as your enemy; the darkness of death
should be as welcome as the light of the sun."

The Spartans were fearsomely effective at close combat.

Spartan guts

An ancient legend told of a young Spartan boy who stole a fox and hid it under his cloak. While the creature was there, it began to gnaw at the boy's stomach. The boy did not cry out, since that would have drawn attention to him. So the fox went on eating, and in the end, the boy collapsed and died of his wounds. The moral of the legend was that he died with his honor intact. If he had publicly hurled the fox away from him, he would have been disgraced—not for stealing but for having been found out. The aim of the Spartan system of military education was to produce men who might show similar courage in times of war.

Mounted Warriors

◄►◄► ◄► ◄► ◄► ◄► ◄► ◄► ◄► ◄► ◄► ◄► ◄► ◄► ◄► ◄► ◄►

Xenophon's *Anabasis* was an eyewitness account of a **mercenary** expedition into the heart of Persia. According to this account, when confronted by the awesome **Persian** cavalry, the Greek infantry took fright, and it had to be explained to them that 10,000 soldiers on horseback were really only 10,000 soldiers: "For no man ever perished in battle from being bitten or kicked by a horse." The soldier on foot could in fact strike harder and with truer aim than the could the soldier on horseback, who had to take great care not to fall off. To most Greeks, until the time of Alexander the Great, horses had little use in battle.

These marble cavalry decorated the Parthenon, which was an Athenian temple built in the middle of the 5th century B.C.E. Note how the riders sit astride their horses without either saddles or stirrups to help keep them balanced.

The drawbacks of horses

Only the rich could afford to keep horses in ancient Greece. Some wealthy warriors rode to battle, then dismounted and fought on foot. This was partly because it was thought that it was nobler to be a foot soldier. It was also because fighting on the backs of small Greek horses was tricky. The rocky, uneven ground was hazardous for horses without horseshoes, and warriors would have had to struggle to sit steadily enough to use swords or *kamaxes*—long, thin spears—since saddles and stirrups had not yet been invented.

In flat regions such as Thessaly, in northern Greece, where horse handling was easier, **cavalry** played an important part in armies. In their distinctive cloaks, tunics, and broad-brimmed hats, Thessalians were known to be the finest horse handlers in Greece. By the early 4th century B.C.E., most city-states had small cavalry forces; horse riders could be used for **reconnaissance** too, as well as to pursue retreating enemies. Then, Alexander made a giant leap forward by using his skillful, swift, highly-trained companion cavalry: by attacking alongside his Macedonian **phalanxes,** which were made up of hoplites, the cavalry had a devastating effect. Alexander also brought back more than 100 elephants on his return from India, but he never got a chance to use them in a **pitched battle.**

Equipping an Athenian cavalry

The cavalry of Athens was expanded to about 1,000 men before the **Peloponnesian** War of 431–404 B.C.E. Each year, the Athenian council inspected horses and warriors both, to check their fitness for service. Horses considered unfit were branded on the jaw with the sign of a wheel. Tomb monuments show that, around this time, a warrior in the Athenian cavalry would have worn sleeveless tunic (like a modern undershirt) under a bronze **cuirass,** with either a wide-brimmed Thessalian-style hat or a hat-shaped helmet on the head, and thin boots on the feet. For weaponry, such a warrior carried a *kamax* and, possibly, a pair of javelins, as well as a cavalry **saber,** which might have had a curved blade.

Lightly-Armed Troops

The hoplites thought that only they fought in a noble, "manly" way. Yet ancient Greek armies often also included lightly armed troops, such as archers, javelin throwers, and stone slingers. In a play by Euripides, a character compared the battle experiences of hoplites and archers: while a hoplite's success depended on the courage of his comrades and while he was left defenseless if his spear broke, an archer could fire up to 10,000 arrows at the enemy and stood far enough away not to be attacked himself.

An ancient Greek archer shows here how he could continue to fight even when he was on the run.

All these lightly armed troops, however, were limited. An archer could actually carry only fifteen to twenty arrows in his carrying case, or quiver, and the firing distance of a Greek bow was only about 260–330 feet (80–100 meters). In addition, the arrows probably could not pierce the hoplites' shields. A javelin thrower could only carry a few javelins, and the distance that they could throw their javelins was no farther than about 70 feet (20 meters). Stone slingers, or slingers of lead "bullets," could do damage, but without a lot of training, they were unlikely to be very accurate. All these types of troops were useful in the attack or defense of city walls, and unlike hoplite **phalanxes,** they did not need to fight on flat ground. When it came to **pitched battles,** hoplites were central throughout the Classical Age, from about 500 B.C.E. until about 300 B.C.E.

Slave warriors

Slaves served their masters on the field of battle just as they did at home. Sometimes called shield bearers or baggage carriers, they personally attended hoplites and **cavalry** during campaigns. They did more than carry equipment, put up tents, and cook food. They might also actually fight as lightly armed troops. Herodotus wrote that, with each Spartan hoplite at the battle of Plataea, in 479 B.C.E., seven lightly armed **Helots** were stationed for the the hoplite's protection. The Spartans even sent whole armies of freed Helots to go on long-distance campaigns in northern Greece and Asia Minor.

Mercenaries

Unlike **citizen**-soldiers, who fought for the honor of their city-states, professional warriors called **mercenaries** fought for pay. There were always mercenaries in the armies of the ancient Greek world, and in the 4th century B.C.E., their numbers became very great. Since their only job was to fight, they were free to take part in long campaigns and in times of peace could practice specialist skills such as archery and javelin throwing. Xenophon, a mercenary commander himself, claimed that, by setting a standard of excellence, mercenary troops improved the quality of the citizen-soldiers with whom they fought. However, there was always the fear that they might desert, for higher pay elsewhere.

Preparing for Battle

Xenophon wrote that a **citizen** must keep himself in good condition for three main reasons: first, to be "ready to serve his state at a moment's notice" as a warrior; second, because "self-preservation also demands it" if he is to survive in war or times of danger; and third, because it was "a disgrace … for a man to grow old without ever seeing the beauty and the strength of which his body is capable."

Here at the *palaestra*, young men exercise under the supervision of a bearded trainer. Two young men wrestle, a third binds his hands for boxing, and a fourth uses a pickax to make the ground softer for when they fall down.

Getting in shape

In most city-states, hoplites were only part-time warriors. For that reason, they could be neither trained nor organized in the manner that modern professional soldiers were. In 5th-century-B.C.E. Athens, citizen **ephebes,** young men

aged eighteen to twenty years, had a basic period of military training. During this they might also man forts or serve in patrols to protect the borders of Athens. For the most part, the main form of training was to exercise in either the *palaestra,* an area for practicing combat sports, or the *gymnasion,* a bigger sports complex. Many Greek men shared Xenophon's views on the value of working out, so this was something that they were happy to do anyway. Some then took additional weapons training from experts.

In Sparta, training was carefully organized for every male citizen. This again centered on athletics but included **drills** with weapons and battle formations, too. The main aim was to fill Sparta's armies with healthy, strong, agile warriors. To this end, Spartans brought up boys in their state **barracks** to make them tough and violent. The boys' food was rationed, so that they were forced to use their wits to steal more. If caught, they were whipped for "stealing unskillfully." Packs of boys competed against each other in vicious ball games and fights. As they approached the age of twenty years, the tests got more severe. During the *krypteia,* or "period of hiding," a boy had to live alone and under cover in the countryside, killing **Helots** who were believed to be dangerous. This training made the Spartans seem invincible when the time came for them to fight in actual battles.

In the gym

The ancient Greeks took sports and exercise very seriously. The greatest athletes of the age won glory at the Olympic Games, as well as at other **Panhellenic** games, and they became legendary idols. No Greek state was permitted to fight during the **truces** that were proclaimed when these games were taking place. Ordinary citizens as well as star athletes could, and did, train at the local *gymnasion.* Those interested in combat sports could practice at the *palaestra.* In the sport of ***pankration,*** you could use any means possible to put your opponent down. In Sparta, even biting and eye-gouging were allowed.

Battle Stations

In ancient Greek warfare, most fighting took place during the four or five months that made up summer. Most campaigns happened between the grain harvest in May and either the grape harvest in September or, at the latest, the November plowing. Summer was also the safest time of year for sailing. Some rich and powerful states, however, tried to gain an advantage by extending this fighting season. Philip of Macedonia, according to Demosthenes, "made no distinction between summer and winter" in the pursuit of his military objectives.

Clash of the phalanxes

Hoplites fought together in **phalanxes.** These were effective only if the ground on which they fought was level, so that they could keep in line. "The Greeks seek out their smoothest piece of ground," wrote Herodotus, "and go down and fight." No army would let another have the advantage of fighting downhill.

Trumpeters signaled the charge. The forces began to walk toward each other, singing a battle song called a *paian*. Gradually they picked up speed, broke into a run, and started whooping instead of singing. Spartan hoplites, however, did not run, but instead, with great discipline, advanced at a steady pace and then halted for a prebattle sacrifice ceremony in front of their enemies.

Greek and **Persian** armies both included trumpeters. Their blasts could signal a battle's start. Music has always played an important part in getting warriors into a fighting mood.

Once the armies clashed, the outcome was mainly decided by how well the hoplites performed on that day. Usually there was little that made the clashing armies different from each other, in either weapons or numbers. Battles might be short, or they might last for most of a day, ending with desperate warriors using even their hands and teeth. When trumpeters sounded the retreat, victory was marked by another singing of the *paian*. Then, at the point where the enemy first turned, a victory "trophy" made from weapons and armor attached to a wooden frame was set up. Meanwhile, pipers would play, and all the victors would give thanks to their gods.

Spartan war preparation

The **biographer** Plutarch's account of the fearsome Spartans' way of going into battle gives some surprising details: "In times of battles the officers relaxed the harshest elements of their discipline, and did not stop the men from beautifying their hair and their armor and their clothing.... They took care over their hair from the time when they were youths, especially seeing to it in times of trouble so that it appeared sleek and well-combed, since ... it makes the handsome better looking and the ugly more frightening.... It was an impressive and frightening sight to see them advancing in time to the flute and leaving no space in the battle-line, with no nervousness in their minds, but calmly and cheerfully moving into the dangerous battle to the sound of music."

Underneath this Spartan warrior's helmet, his hair would have been very neat. According to the historian Herodotus, Spartans groomed themselves "so that they might die with their heads tidy."

Tilting the Balance in Battle

Xenophon believed that a military commander should "devise a **ruse** for every occasion, since in war nothing is more profitable than deceit…. Think about successes in war, and you will find that most of the greatest have been achieved by means of deceit." He may have been stretching his point a little. Once two hoplite armies had started to slug it out there was little a general could do, except to fight well himself, as an example to his men.

This is a picture from the Middle Ages of the great Greek scientist and engineer Archimedes, who lived from about 287 until 212 B.C.E. He tried to help to defend Syracuse by inventing cranes to lift enemy ships and turn them upside down and by using mirrors to focus the Sun's rays on the ships and set them on fire.

Stealing a march on the enemy

Sometimes armies tried to capture a city by siege—in other words, by camping around it and forcing the **citizens** to surrender. There was always room for some **ingenuity** here. An improved scaling ladder was invented to make it easier for attackers to climb city walls, and another ladder, which was fitted with a shield, allowed men who stood on it to make observations for longer periods of time. Burning missiles might be thrown at a city to set fire to its defenses, and the Athenians used battering rams to attack Samos in 440 B.C.E. Meanwhile, great **catapults** were devised to keep enemy siege engines at bay. Surviving records show that the Greeks carefully calculated the distance that missiles could be fired.

On the field of battle, few tactical thinkers were greater than Epaminondas of Thebes. At the battle of Leuctra, in 371 B.C.E., the Thebans had to face a Spartan-led army. The Spartans usually put their best troops on the right wing. They expected to win an advantage there and then to wheel inward and "roll up" the rest of the enemy line. For that reason, their plan was to win the battle before the less-skilled troops at the left wing and the center could get involved and lose it. Epaminondas responded by arranging his Theban hoplites in a column 50 ranks deep, which was not a very wide formation. Then his column struck on the left, broke through the elite Spartan right wing, and won the battle before the lesser Theban troops could lose it. This may sound like a simple plan now, but it needed great skill and discipline to carry out in the heat of battle.

Hannibal's sneaky snakes

The great general Hannibal, who lived from 247 to 183 B.C.E., led Carthage in a great war against the Romans. Once, he was in charge of a **Hellenistic** fleet. According to the Roman Cornelius Nepos, he sent his sailors ashore to collect live poisonous snakes. When the snakes were brought back, Hannibal had them sealed into fragile jars, then fired into the ships of the enemy. The men of the enemy fleet surely would have panicked to find the snakes escaping among them and would have lost concentration for the battle ahead.

Fighting Ships

The earliest Greek warships were used just to transport warriors, not to fight against other ships. After about 700 B.C.E., fights at sea began, and ships carried soldiers to board other ships or to defend their own ship. The *trireme* became the most important Greek warship. It had sails but was mainly powered by rowers and instead of just one line of them, as in earlier vessels, a *trireme* had three banks of up to 50 oarsmen. They were all crammed into a space about 120 feet (37 meters) long by 20 feet (6 meters) wide. The *trireme* was easily **maneuverable** and could travel at the fast speed of 7 nautical miles per hour (13 kilometers per hour).

A modern reconstruction of an ancient Greek *trireme*. There were two masts, from which sails could be unfurled when there was a good, strong wind.

All aboard

Athenian *triremes* were like worlds in miniature. The *trierarch*, or captain, was a wealthy **citizen** who either had volunteered or had been appointed to the job. Under him served the **marines:** usually ten citizen hoplites, four archers, and the ship's specialist officers (a helmsman, a lookout, a rowing master, a pipe player, a **purser,** and a shipwright for emergency repairs). Then there were all the oarsmen: these could be lower-class citizens, slaves, foreigners, or anyone willing to serve for pay. The hoplites on board may have looked down on the more **menial** oarsmen. However, these professional rowers proved to be far more valuable than did inexperienced citizens who took up oars in time of war.

Masters of the sea

In the early years of the **Peloponnesian** War (431–404 B.C.E.), Athens kept 100 ships on semipermanent guard duty and often employed up to 250 ships in total, with up to 50,000 men on board. Clearly the Athenians thought it was vital to maintain a powerful presence on the seas. So did the other city-states.

These *triremes* not only carried out blockades and engaged in **pitched battles,** but also made sure that food supplies in merchant vessels could be safely shipped from the Black Sea. As the *Constitution of Athens* says, "If a city is rich in wood for shipbuilding, where will it be able to dispose of it without the permission of the ruler of the sea? And the same is true of iron or bronze or sailcloth, which very things are what ships are made of. And those who rule the sea can say where they are to go." For these reasons alone, the city-states competed for what was called *thalassocracy*, or mastery of the seas.

Naval Warfare

◄► ◄► ◄► ◄► ◄► ◄► ◄► ◄► ◄► ◄► ◄► ◄► ◄► ◄► ◄► ◄► ◄►

One of the greatest naval battles took place at Salamis in 480 B.C.E., during the **Persian** wars. After defeat on land at Thermopylae, the government of Athens evacuated the city's women and children and then sent its male **citizens** to man the *triremes*. On receipt of a false message that the *triremes* were trying to flee, the Persian fleet tried to prevent the *triremes* from escaping by blocking a narrow channel between the Greek mainland and the island of Salamis.

This was, however, just what the Athenians wanted. The lighter Greek *triremes* were in fact waiting to attack the Persians, in a place where it would be hard for them to **maneuver.** In the end, the Persians lost almost all their ships in a crushing defeat. Some of the victors may soon have been among a theater audience listening to actors who celebrated the great event in a play by Aeschylus. With relish, the playwright described how, at the battle's end, the Greeks "beat the Persians with splintered oars and planks from wrecked ships," as if they were beating to death shoals of fish that had been caught in a net: "Moans and shrieks sounded across the sea."

This decoration shows ancient Greek sea warfare, about 500 B.C.E.

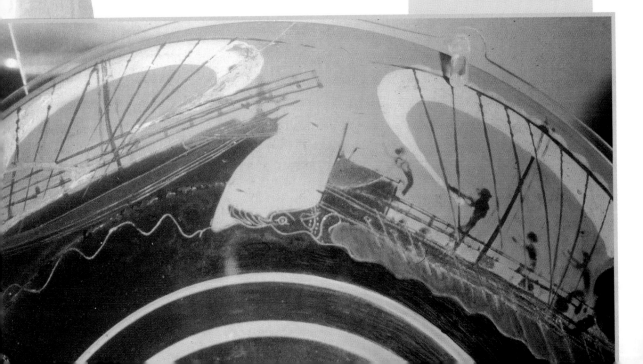

Trireme tactics

For a **pitched battle** at sea, *triremes* had to be **deployed** in a single line to face the enemy. When the two lines came close enough, the men on board might engage in what Athenian historian Thucydides called the "old style" of combat: the *triremes* lay still, while the warriors launched missiles or tried to enter and seize the closest enemy vessel. The newer style involved maneuvering quickly to get beside an enemy *trireme* and then smashing into it with the heavy, pointed, bronze-sheathed ram on the lower part of the attacking *trireme's* **prow.** A quick withdrawal was then vital, leaving the enemy in chaos—and hopefully throwing the whole enemy line into confusion. The eventual winners would sing a *paian,* or battle song, and would then build a victory trophy from weapons and armor on the nearest island, just as hoplite victors did.

Themistocles was the Athenian politician who masterminded the victory over the Persians at Salamis in 480 B.C.E. He had also persuaded the Athenians to build more warships in the years leading up to this battle. The enlarged fleet, he said, would be "wooden walls" to keep Athens safe.

The Cost of War

Warfare has always been an expensive business. In ancient Greece, it cost more to wage war than it did to finance any other public activity—including most massive building projects, such as the building of the Acropolis in Athens. There was also, after each war, the great cost of repairing all the damage that had been done to the cities and the countryside. Before the Classical Age, private individuals paid for most campaigns. Then the city-states, funded by **citizens'** taxes, took on the financial burden. In time, the winners of wars tended to be the states with the greater wealth.

Who paid the bill?

There were three main ways to pay for military campaigns: first, by using public funds; second, by seizing **loot** from the enemy while the marching along (in other words, by making the campaigns pay for themselves); and third, by making somewhat shameful deals with wealthy **barbarian** states.

Sieges could take a long time and could be very expensive for the besieging army. Thasos and Plataea both managed to resist their attackers for more than two *years*. Many cities were captured when traitors inside betrayed the defenders.

In 483 B.C.E., the Athenians decided to create a state-owned navy, by using money from taxes. Rowers and **marines** were offered pay at a fixed daily rate. Later, hoplites and their servants were paid at the same rate, and so were **cavalry.** Maintenance of the navy was especially expensive, and so were the sieges in which paid hoplites took part. The nine-month siege of Samos cost the Athenians more than 1,200 **talents** of silver. Afterward, in 431 B.C.E., there were only 6,000 *talents* left in the whole Athenian treasury. Less wealthy states could not have coped.

The cost of a hoplite

Hoplites had to pay for their own arms and armor, their bedding, and a few days' rations of bread, cheese, onions, or salted fish. When they were in friendly territory, the local people might help them out. When they entered enemy territory, they would help themselves to whatever they needed. Therefore, Greek armies did not need many supplies or big stocks of ammunition and often traveled with a small baggage train or group of pack animals only. All this changed if a siege had to be carried out. Then, an army needed siege engines to be brought up, as well as plenty of supplies for the waiting warriors.

A second way to raise funds was to seize **plunder** during the fighting. Merchant ships, fishing boats, or passenger ferries might be captured. On land, dealers in **booty** might sell prisoners or cattle that had been taken, and prisoners of war might be kept for ransom. This all brought money in, but there was no way to know in advance how much. The third source of income was more reliable. In the **Peloponnesian** War, both Athens and Sparta begged **Persian** governors and generals to **subsidize** them with gold. With the backing of this former enemy, the Spartans triumphed.

Limiting the Damage

The human cost of warfare in ancient Greece might be very high. Many wars were short and had few long-term effects, but some were devastating. The modern historian Hans van Wees calculates that during the Classical Age about 24 city-states were **annihilated:** "The enemy cut the throats of the entire adult male population, made slaves of the women, children and elderly, and sold to new masters those who were slaves already.... Thousands more died in each of the major battles of the age.... Soldiers fell at the rate of one in seven on the losing side, one in twenty among the victors."

What limits did the Greeks themselves put on all this devastation? For one thing, the fighting season could be confined to four or five months of each year. For another, fighting was supposed to be suspended for religious reasons during certain sacred periods. The Spartans actually refused to take part in the battle of Marathon, since for religious reasons they were not allowed to start a campaign before the full moon. The superstitious Greeks also tried to predict, by observing the world around them, whether or not it was wise to fight.

One warrior has already fallen in this battle. Many Greeks held the view that it was better to die nobly than to survive by being cowardly.

Interpreting the omens

The trouble with omens was that their meaning might be unclear. The **biographer** Plutarch described a **nocturnal eclipse** of the Moon that happened just before an Athenian night operation against their enemy: "The men were convinced that it must be a supernatural **portent** and a warning from the gods that fearful calamities were at hand." There was no experienced **soothsayer** in the army to give a verdict. *Was it really an evil omen, or "was it a positive advantage, since an operation of this kind … needs concealment above all else, while light is fatal to it"?* The commander decided to take no chances and held back his men on that night.

At the ancient Olympic Games, one race was run in full armor. A three-month-long sacred **truce** was proclaimed when the Games took place, so that even warring city-states could still send athletes to take part.

After the battle

In later classical times, when a Greek city was captured, the victors were not supposed to massacre the people inside, nor were they to destroy the buildings. After a battle, it was forbidden to mutilate the dead bodies of the enemy. The victors were allowed to strip the bodies of all their possessions, and then the corpses could be taken back by their comrades. However, rules such as these were not always observed. In 405 B.C.E., at the end of the **Peloponnesian** War, about 3,000 captured Athenians were executed. This was because earlier the Athenians had voted to cut off the hands of all their prisoners of war and, on capturing warships from Corinth and Andros, had simply thrown both crews overboard.

How Do We Know? Vergina

For centuries, ancient Greece was disunited. **Polis** often fought against *polis*; the many states pulled together only when there was a common threat from abroad. Then, Macedonia, a warlike state in the north of the Greek-speaking world, grew mightier than all the rest. The king of Macedonia, Philip II, conquered the whole of Greece and brought to an end the era of the city-state. His son Alexander then expanded the new Macedonian Empire far into Asia. This was the last great achievement of ancient Greek civilization.

Here we see what Vergina looks like today—a ghost of the military city that once served as the capital under the mighty king Philip of Macedonia.

Coarse, barbaric Macedonians?

In the 1970s, excavations began at Pella, the Macedonian capital after Aigai. Some of the **artifacts** discovered were the spoils of battles. Women were buried with gold jewelry, while men were buried with elaborate swords. There were also marble sculptures, terra-cotta **statuettes,** and bronze **figurines** of the Greek gods and goddesses. Experts used to believe that the Macedonians were a coarse, military people with little interest in the finer things. These beautiful finds show that they were not just the most effective and successful warriors of ancient Greek times. When not campaigning, they and their families led luxurious, refined lives.

The tomb of King Philip

Information about Philip of Macedon comes from archaeological evidence in addition to ancient books. His capital was at a place called Aigai, which later came to be known as Vergina. In 1977, archaeologists opened up Philip's royal tomb there. In ancient times, people were often buried with their prized possessions. At Vergina, the archaeologists found an ivory head that is probably meant to be an image of Philip. Other finds inside his beautifully painted tomb included a golden crown, a golden quiver for arrows, and silver bowls and cups. In addition, pieces of bronze armor were found, including a pair of bronze **greaves.** Because one was shorter than the other and because ancient eyewitnesses had written that the king limped from a war wound, archaeologists think that they may have once belonged to Philip. It is not surprising that so many of the prized possessions of such a successful soldier were connected with weapons and warfare.

Greece today is littered with many such ancient sites. **Excavations** by archaeologists may dig up all sorts of hidden treasures—and may help historians to form a clearer picture of a time when warfare was such a regular part of life.

Timeline

All the following dates are B.C.E.:

c. 3000–c. 1450	Greece is controlled by Minoan kings from Crete.
c. 1600–c. 1100	Greek-speaking Mycenaeans rule separate kingdoms in mainland Greece.
c. 1100–c. 800	Greece goes through a period of wars and migration.
c. 800–c. 700	Homer's *Iliad* and *Odyssey* were probably written; Greece is made up of small city-states that are ruled by separate kings or noble familie
c. 750–c. 550	Greeks set up colonies in lands around the Mediterranean Sea.
c. 500	Some city-states become democracies; of these, Athens is the most powerful.
c. 490–479	The main period of **Persian** invasions of Greece occurs.
431–404	The **Peloponnesian** War, between Greek city-states, ends with Sparta eclipsing Athens as the most powerful state in mainland Greece.
378–371	Sparta is eclipsed by a new power, Thebes.
336–323	Greece is ruled by Alexander the Great of Macedon after his invasion and conquest.
146	Greece becomes part of the Roman Empire.

More Books to Read

Barron's Educational Editors. *Greek Life.* Hauppage, N.Y.: Barron's Educational Services, Inc., 1998.

Bartole, Mira, and Christine Ronan. *Ancient Greece.* Parsippany, N.J.: Pearson Learning, 1995.

Clare, John D., ed., *Ancient Greece.* New York: Harcourt Children's Books, 1994.

Coolidge, Olivia E. *The Trojan War.* New York: Houghton Mifflin Co., 2001. An older reader can help you with this book.

Day, Nancy. *Your Travel Guide to Ancient Greece.* Minneapolis: Lerner Publishing Group, 2000. An older reader can help you with this book.

Ganeri, Anita. *Ancient Greeks.* Danbury, Conn.: Franklin Watts, 1993.

Malam, John. *A Greek Town.* Danbury, Conn.: Franklin Watts, 1999.

Nardo, Don. *Life in Ancient Greece.* Farmington Hills, Mich.: The Gale Group, 1996. An older reader can help you with this book.

Pearson, Anne. *Ancient Greece.* New York: Dorling-Kindersley Publishers, Inc., 2000.

Rees, Rosemary. *The Ancient Greeks.* Chicago: Heinemann Library, 1997.

Glossary

annihilated destroyed, wiped out

aristocrats nobles who were considered, often on the basis of wealth, to be the best citizens in a state

artifact item, useful or artistic, made by a person

autocratic governed by a single powerful ruler

barbarian anyone who was not Greek

barracks building or buildings in which soldiers live apart from other people

besieged surrounded and made to surrender, often because those within the city would finally starve over the course of the long siege

biographer writer of the stories of others' lives

booty items seized and kept in times of war (other words for this are "loot" and "plunder")

casualty person who is killed or injured in warfare or an accident

catapult a military device for the hurling of missiles, often used in sieges

cavalry part of an army that goes into battle on horseback

citizen person with the right to take part in politics, in particular, by voting

civilization distinct way of life that is common to a particular group of people

corselet armor that covered the trunk of the body

cuirass pieces of armor (breastplate and back piece) fastened together to protect a soldier's body

democracy method of government by which citizens can elect their own rulers

deployed organized in battle formation

drill exercise to train soldiers to act as a team and follow orders

ephebes Athenian men aged eighteen to twenty years, on military service

excavated dug up to be examined by archaeologists

excavation dig site where archaeologists work

figurine statuettes, small figure

greaves pieces of armor that protected the shins

Hellenistic Greek influenced, or in the Greek style (from the Greek word *"Hellen,"* meaning a Greek)

Helot one of the conquered people who worked for the Spartans

hubris pride that leads to punishment by the gods

infantry part of an army that goes into battle on foot

ingenuity cleverness, quick-wittedness

loot items seized and kept in times of war (other words for this are "booty" and "plunder")

majordomo chief official in a royal household

maneuverable easy to move about

maneuver to plan and control a movement

marine soldier trained to serve on land or sea

menial low-level

mercenary soldier who fights purely for pay

morale confidence and enthusiasm

nocturnal eclipse passage of one heavenly body (planet or star) in front of another, at night

orally in spoken form

orator public speaker

Panhellenic relating to the whole of Greece and all its people

pankration ferocious Olympic combat sport

Peloponnese southern region of mainland Greece. This region includes the city-state of Sparta

Persian person who lived in the ancient Middle Eastern kingdom of Persia, which is now known as Iran

phalanx group of soldiers banded tightly together for battle

philosopher person interested in thoughts and theories, from the Greek words meaning lover of knowledge

pike thrusting weapon that is similar to a spear

pitched battle battle in which the time and place are arranged beforehand

plunder items seized and kept in times of war (other words for this are "booty" and "loot")

polis (more than one are called *poleis*) Greek city-state

portent omen

prow front of a ship

purser officer who keeps accounts on board a ship

reconnaissance checking out the "lie of the land" and the enemy's position

ruse trick

saber sword worn by cavalry that has a curved blade

soothsayer someone who can foretell the future

stalemate tied battle, with neither side winning

statuette small statue, usually of a person

steed horse, especially one used in warfare

subsidize give financial assistance, help to pay the cost of something

talent very large unit of Greek money (6 *obols* = 1 *drachma*; 100 *drachmas* = 1 *mina*; 60 *minas* = 1 *talent*)

truce time during which fighting was temporarily stopped

Index